Don't Turn Your Back On Me II Book AND Workbook

In English AND Spanish,

ACKNOWLEDGEMENT

I Would Like To Acknowledge The CREATOR OF
HEAVEN AND EARTH (GOD) FOR ALL THAT HE HAS
Given Me. Thanking God I Am For My Talents and
Gifts.
I Recognize That The Lord Gave Me This Gift,
Which Allows Me To Share With Children And
Everyone That Participates In The Reading Of The
Literary Material That I Produce Through The
Commission Of God.
Thank You Lord God
I Will Forever Be Grateful
For Your Trust In Me

Pamela Denise Brown
Goodwill Ambassador
For The Positive Cultivation Of Children

My EDUCATIONAL Collection Of Books Are For The
Advancement Of Children.
I'm Not Selling Books, I Am However, Providing
Thought Leading Reinforcements, That Can Be
Simplistically Utilized As Reference Material,
As An Investment In The Positive Cultivation Of
Children's Lives.

A little information about the author. I write EDUCATIONAL books to educate children, to transform the way a child thinks, to better children so they can become successful people. I write EDUCATIONAL books to help children develop and grow psychologically. As an Ambassador for the cultivation of children, I am a trusted source moving to inspire children by urging children to be open to new ways of thinking in how to deal with others and differences. I present children with an opportunity to replicate and scale the ideas from the pages of the encouraging literature I produce, into sustainable change, thereby shaping the lives of children from any background, community, age, ethnicity or gender. My goal is to give children balance and broaden their understanding of humanity as it relates to "co-existing" in society as a coherent whole. I have codified what I know and placed it within reach. I am strategically reaching into the mind of every child that reads the literary information that I have produced.

Books Speak For You books may be ordered through booksellers or by contacting:
Booksspeakforyou.com
The views expressed in this work are solely those of the author.
Any illustration provided by iStock and such images are being used for illustrative purposes.
Certain stock imagery © iStock.
ISBN: 978-1640503502
Library of Congress Control Number: 2017906164
Printed in the United States Of America

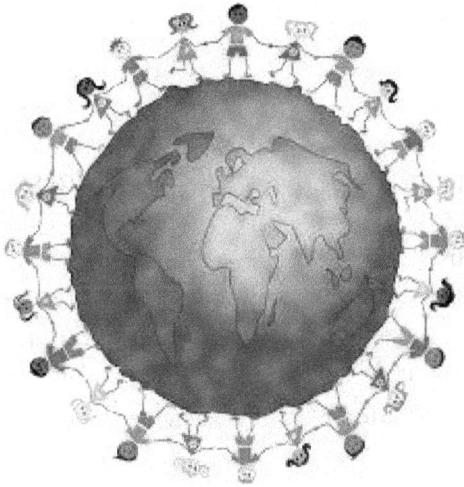

I Dedicate This Book To Every Child With Love In Countries Around The World

- A

- Afghanistan
- Albania
- Algeria
- Andorra
- Angola
- Antigua and Barbuda
- Argentina
- Armenia
- Australia
- Austria
- Azerbaijan
- B
- Bahamas

- Bahrain
- Bangladesh
- Barbados
- Belarus
- Belgium
- Belize
- Benin
- Bhutan
- Bolivia
- Bosnia and Herzegovina
- Botswana
- Brazil
- Brunei
- Bulgaria
- Burkina Faso
- Burundi
- C
- Cabo Verde
- Cambodia
- Cameroon
- Canada
- Central African Republic (CAR)
- Chad
- Chile
- China
- Colombia
- Comoros
- Democratic Republic of the Congo
- Republic of the Congo
- Costa Rica
- Cote d'Ivoire
- Croatia
- Cuba
- Cyprus
- Czech Republic
- D
- Denmark
- Djibouti
- Dominica
- Dominican Republic
- E
- Ecuador
- Egypt
- El Salvador
- Equatorial Guinea
- Eritrea
- Estonia
- Ethiopia
- F
- Fiji
- Finland
- France
- G
- Gabon

- Gambia
- Georgia
- Germany
- Ghana
- Greece
- Grenada
- Guatemala
- Guinea
- Guinea-Bissau
- Guyana

- H
- Haiti
- Honduras
- Hungary
- I
- Iceland
- India
- Indonesia
- Iran
- Iraq
- Ireland
- Israel
- Italy
- J
- Jamaica
- Japan
- Jordan
- K
- Kazakhstan
- Kenya

- Kiribati
- Kosovo
- Kuwait
- Kyrgyzstan
- L
- Laos
- Latvia
- Lebanon
- Lesotho
- Liberia
- Libya
- Liechtenstein
- Lithuania
- Luxembourg
- M
- Macedonia
- Madagascar
- Malawi
- Malaysia
- Maldives
- Mali
- Malta
- Marshall Islands
- Mauritania
- Mauritius
- Mexico
- Micronesia
- Moldova
- Monaco
- Mongolia
- Montenegro

- Morocco
- Mozambique
- Myanmar (Burma)
- N
- Namibia
- Nauru
- Nepal
- Netherlands
- New Zealand
- Nicaragua
- Niger
- Nigeria
- North Korea
- Norway
- O
- Oman
- P
- Pakistan
- Palau
- Palestine
- Panama
- Papua New Guinea
- Paraguay
- Peru
- Philippines
- Poland
- Portugal

- Q
- Qatar

- R
- Romania
- Russia
- Rwanda
- S
- St. Kitts and Nevis
- St. Lucia
- St. Vincent and the Grenadines
- Samoa
- San Marino
- Sao Tome and Principe
- Saudi Arabia
- Senegal
- Serbia
- Seychelles
- Sierra Leone
- Singapore
- Slovakia
- Slovenia
- Solomon Islands
- Somalia
- South Africa
- South Korea
- South Sudan
- Spain
- Sri Lanka
- Sudan
- Suriname
- Swaziland

- Sweden
- Switzerland
- Syria
- T
- Taiwan
- Tajikistan
- Tanzania
- Thailand
- Timor-Leste
- Togo
- Tonga
- Trinidad and Tobago
- Tunisia
- Turkey
- Turkmenistan
- Tuvalu
- U
- Uganda
- Ukraine
- United Arab Emirates (UAE)
- United Kingdom (UK)
- United States of America (USA)
- Uruguay
- Uzbekistan
- V
- Vanuatu
- Vatican City (Holy See)
- Venezuela
- Vietnam
- Y
- Yemen
- Z
- Zambia
- Zimbabwe

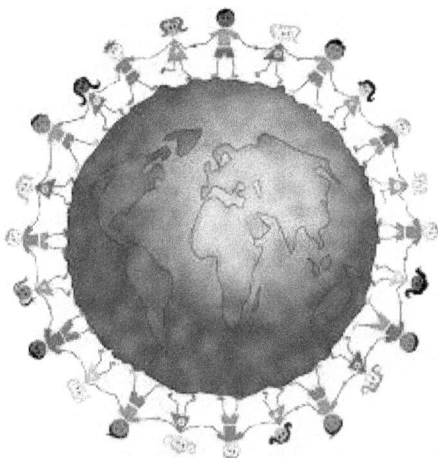

ANOTHER
SPECIAL DEDICATION TO ALL THE
CHILDREN WITH LOVE
IN CITIES IN THE
UNITED STATES OF AMERICA

Albany, NY
Albuquerque, NM
Anchorage, AK
Annapolis, MD
Atlanta, GA
Atlantic City, NJ
Augusta, ME
Austin, TX
Bakersfield, CA
Baltimore, MD
Baton Rouge, LA
Billings, MT
Biloxi, MS
Bismarck, ND
Bloomsburg, PA
Boise, ID
Boston, MA
Buffalo, NY
Burlington, VT
Carson City, NV
Charleston, SC
Charleston, WV
Charlotte, NC
Charlottesville, VA
Cheyenne, WY
Chicago, IL
Chicago, IL
Cleveland, OH
Colorado Springs, CO
Columbia, SC
Columbus, OH
Concord, CA
Concord, NH
Corpus Christi, TX

Dallas, TX
Davenport, IA
Daytona, FL
Denver, CO
Des Moines, IA
Des Plaines, IL
Detroit, MI
Dover, DE
Durham, NC
Erie, PA
Eugene, OR
Fayetteville, NC
Flagstaff, AZ
Frankfort, KY
Ft. Lauderdale, FL
Gettysburg, PA
Greenville, SC
Hampton Roads, VA
Harrisburg, PA
Hartford, CT
Helena, MT
Hollywood, CA
Honolulu, HI
Houston, TX
Huntsville, AL
Indianapolis, IN
Jackson, MS
Jackson Hole-Grand
Tetons, WY
Jacksonville, FL
Jefferson City, MO
Jim Thorpe, PA
Juneau, AK
Kansas City, MO

Knoxville, TN	Newark, NJ
Lake Tahoe, NV	Niagara Falls, NY
Lancaster, PA	Northville, MI
Lancaster / Central PA	Oklahoma City, OK
Lansing, MI	Orlando, FL
Las Vegas, NV	Olympia, WA
Las Vegas, NV	Omaha, NE
Lexington, KY	Orange County, CA
Lincoln, NE	Palm Springs, CA
Little Rock, AR	Pensacola, FL
Long Island, NY	Philadelphia, PA
Los Angeles, CA	Phoenix, AZ
Los Angeles, CA	Pierre, SD
Louisville, KY	Pittsburgh, PA
Madison, WI	Portland, ME
Manchester, NH	Portland, OR
Maryville, TN	Providence, RI
Memphis, TN	Pueblo, CO
Miami, FL	Raleigh, NC
Miami, FL	Rapid City, SD
Milwaukee, WI	Reno, NV
Minneapolis, MN	Richmond, VA
Mobile, AL	Sacramento, CA
Montgomery, AL	Salt Lake City, UT
Montpelier, VT	San Diego, CA
Morrison, IL	San Francisco, CA
Nashville, TN	Santa Cruz, CA
New Haven, CT	Santa Fe, NM
New Orleans, LA	Scranton, PA
New York: Bronx	Seattle, WA
New York: Brooklyn	Sedona, AZ
New York: Manhattan	Shreveport, LA
New York: Queens	Silicon Valley, CA
New York City	Springfield, IL

St. Joseph, MO
St. Paul, MN
St. Louis, MO
State College, PA
SurfScranton, PA
Syracuse, NY
Tacoma, WA
Tallahassee, FL
Tampa, FL
Topeka, KS
Trenton, NJ
Tulsa, OK
Tuscon, AZ
Tyler, TX
Washington, DC
Wichita, KS
Wilkes-Barre, PA
Williamsburg, VA
Williamsport, PA
Wilmington, DE
Yuma, AZ

INTRODUCTION

My Collection Of EDUCATIONAL Books are designed to foster the social development of children psychologically. My books are designed to teach children values and morals and reintroduce them to manners.

I believe the books I write will transform the minds of children, which ultimately will cause them to pause, to think and make better choices.

My EDUCATIONAL Books are designed to effectuate change and influence success in the lives of every child.

The EDUCATIONAL Books in the Collection are Reinforcements to Learning.

My EDUCATIONAL books will help build children's self-esteem and confidence to a level that will help them socially engage in a diverse world with confidence and harmony and ultimately prepare them for life.

Children Stand Silently Trying To
Open Doors That Cannot Be
Opened With Hands
Written 11/23/2015 11:18 a.m.

If To Educate Is Your Objective Than To
Learn Is Your Aim
Written 11/21/2015 1:41 a.m.

With Even Strokes Caress The
Mind,

With Gentle Words Handle A Child,

With Excitement Finish The Race,

With Commitment Help A Child

Stay In Place

LOVE IS EVERLASTING WITH GOD

Written: July 3, 2016 @ 10:06 pm.

If You Really Want To Enhance The LIFE Of A Child, Your First Step Is To See Yourself Like A Child And Then Approach The Child Like You See Yourself

Written: 11/21/2015 2:22 a.m.

If You're In A Crowed Room And A Child Is Sitting Alone, That Can Only Mean The Room Is Empty

Written 11/21/2015 1:42 a.m.

DON'T
TURN YOUR
BACK
ON ME II
ENGLISH

DON'T TURN YOUR BACK
ON ME

To me it's a sign of rejection. No one wants to feel rejected.

To feel rejected is:

REJECTED (reject): to refuse or consider: something that is not good enough for some purpose, a person who is not accepted or liked by other people.

DON'T TURN YOUR BACK

ON ME

When you turn your back on me I feel confused.

To feel confused is:

CONFUSED: unable to think clear; bewildered.

DON'T TURN YOUR BACK

ON ME

I feel like I don't belong, I feel out of place and I don't like to feel like I don't belong.

To feel like I don't belong is the opposite of belong:

To belong is:

BELONG: to feel like a part of a particular group, organization or class.

Not to belong makes me feel like I'm not a part of my community or family.

DON'T TURN YOUR BACK
ON ME

It's a sign that you don't want to hear what I have to say and to me that's being rude.

To be rude is:

RUDE: not having or showing concern or respect for the rights and feelings of other people: not polite.

DON'T TURN YOUR BACK

ON ME

It screams you don't care.

We should all care about each other.

To care for someone is:

CARE: to feel interest in something: to be interested in or concerned about something, to feel affection for someone.

DON'T TURN YOUR BACK

ON ME

When you do this you make me feel like I'm not important.

My thoughts are important to me and so are my views.

To be important is:

IMPORTANT: having serious meaning or worth: deserving or requiring serious attention.

DON'T TURN YOUR BACK
ON ME

When you turn your back on me I feel Isolated.

To feel isolated is to feel:

ISOLATED: separated from others.

DON'T TURN YOUR BACK ON ME

Please don't turn your back on me, you make me feel like you're unapproachable. I feel like I'm a stranger. I don't want to feel like a stranger when I'm around people that are supposed to care for me. I don't want to feel like I can't approach the person that is suppose to help me.

To be unapproachable is:

UNAPPROACHABLE: not welcoming or friendly.

DON'T TURN YOUR BACK
ON ME

I asked you not To Turn Your Back On Me, every time you do this, I feel withdrawn.

When I feel withdrawn, I feel like this:

WITHDRAWN: removed from immediate contact or easy approach:

DON'T TURN YOUR BACK

ON ME

I feel ashamed. Why should I feel ashamed? I didn't do anything wrong.

When you make me feel ashamed, you make me feel like this:

ASHAMED: feeling shame or guilt: not wanting to do something, because of embarrassment.

DON'T TURN YOUR BACK

ON ME

It makes me angry.   I'd rather
be happy.

When you make me feel angry,
I feel like this:

ANGRY: having a strong feeling
of being upset or annoyed.

DON'T TURN YOUR BACK

ON ME

It makes me unstable. I want to be stable, especially in my mind. I want to be sure of myself.

When you make me feel unstable, I feel like this:

UNSTABLE: not emotionally or mentally healthy; not held in a secure position.

DON'T TURN YOUR BACK

ON ME

I feel helpless. If I'm helpless I can't defend myself.

When I feel helpless, this is how I feel:

HELPLESS: not protected: not able to defend yourself: unable to do something to make a situation, task, etc, better or easier.

DON'T TURN YOUR BACK

ON ME

I don't feel wanted. I want to be wanted and I want people to want to be around me.

To be wanted is to feel:

WANTED: Something that is desired or needed.

DON'T TURN YOUR BACK

ON ME

I become traumatized. I'm traumatized when you turn your back on me and sometimes I can't get it together.

When I feel traumatized I feel like this:

TRAUMATIZED: to cause (someone) to become very upset in a way that often leads to serious emotional problems: to cause someone to suffer.

DON'T TURN YOUR BACK

ON ME

Every time you do this, I care less and less about things that should matter to me.

To care about a person is to:

CARE: to feel interest in something: to be interested in or concerned about something: to feel affection for someone: to want to do something or to be something.

DON'T TURN YOUR BACK

ON ME

It jeopardizes the respect we should have for one another.

I'm taught to respect everyone.

I want to be respected and I want respect.

RESPECT: is: a feeling of admiring someone or something that is good, valuable, important, etc.

DON'T TURN YOUR BACK

ON ME

Every time you do this to me I lose interest in you. I don't want to lose interest.

To have interest in someone means to:

INTEREST: to cause (someone) to want to learn more about something or to become involved in something. To persuade (someone) to have, take, or participate in (something).

DON'T TURN YOUR BACK

ON ME

It makes me feel like I don't matter, like I don't count. I feel like I am not in the room.

To Matter is:

MATTER: to be important.

DON'T TURN YOUR BACK
ON ME

When you turn your back on me, I feel hurt. I don't want to feel hurt. I don't want to feel pain. When you hurt someone you cause them grief.

To hurt someone is to cause physical pain or injury to them.

HURT: means to cause emotional pain or anguish, it means to offend.

DON'T TURN YOUR BACK
ON ME

Whenever someone turns their back on me, I feel like I was left alone.

To be alone is to be:

ALONE: without anyone or anything else: not involving or including anyone or anything else: separate from other people or things: feeling unhappy, because of being separated from other people.

DON'T TURN YOUR BACK

ON ME

Whenever you turn your back on me, I feel like I don't fit in. I want to fit in and I want to be liked.

To fit in is to be socially compatible with other members of a group or people.

DON'T TURN YOUR BACK ON ME!!!

HEY GUYS

HERE ARE SOME QUESTIONS

Has anyone ever turned their back on you? (a parent, a teacher, a friend or a relative)

_____

_____

If yes, how did it make you feel?

Try to use words that best describe your feelings and accurate emotions.

Use this space to write down how you really felt when someone turned his or her back on you. Be honest.

_____

_____

_____

_____

_____

Now it's time for the switch. If you have ever turned your back on anyone and they expressed how they felt. Below, write down how you made that person feel and how you felt after they told you how they felt.

_____

_____

_____

_____

_____

_____

_____

_____

_____

_____

_____

_____

Have you ever treated someone different because they were not like you?

_____

_____

_____

_____

_____

_____

_____

_____

_____

_____

_____

_____

_____

_____

Make a list of good emotions.

_____

_____

_____

_____

_____

_____

_____

_____

_____

_____

_____

_____

_____

_____

_____

Write down a list of things that make you feel sad, withdrawn, rejected or unwanted.

_____

_____

_____

_____

_____

_____

_____

_____

_____

_____

_____

_____

_____

_____

Thank You

For Purchasing This Book
In Your Purchase,

You Are Celebrating
With Me,

The Completion Of One
Of God's Many Works
Through Me.

Contact Information
1-800-757-0598

Website: Booksspeakforyou.com

Email:
Booksspeakforyou@yahoo.com

Share Your Story

Share Your Dream

This Is The Letter The President Sent To Me Thanking Me For Inspiring Our Next Generation Of Doers, Dreamers And Thinkers... I Was Inspired

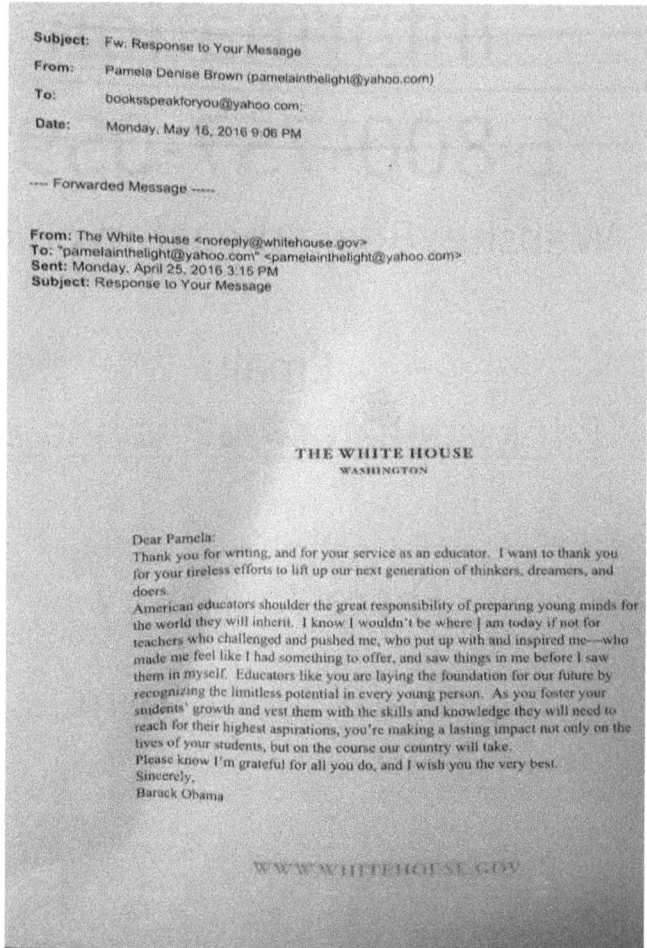

Subject: Fw: Response to Your Message
From: Pamela Denise Brown (pamelainthelight@yahoo.com)
To: booksspeakforyou@yahoo.com;
Date: Monday, May 16, 2016 9:06 PM

---- Forwarded Message ----

From: The White House <noreply@whitehouse.gov>
To: "pamelainthelight@yahoo.com" <pamelainthelight@yahoo.com>
Sent: Monday, April 25, 2016 3:15 PM
Subject: Response to Your Message

THE WHITE HOUSE
WASHINGTON

Dear Pamela:

Thank you for writing, and for your service as an educator. I want to thank you for your tireless efforts to lift up our next generation of thinkers, dreamers, and doers.

American educators shoulder the great responsibility of preparing young minds for the world they will inherit. I know I wouldn't be where I am today if not for teachers who challenged and pushed me, who put up with and inspired me—who made me feel like I had something to offer, and saw things in me before I saw them in myself. Educators like you are laying the foundation for our future by recognizing the limitless potential in every young person. As you foster your students' growth and vest them with the skills and knowledge they will need to reach for their highest aspirations, you're making a lasting impact not only on the lives of your students, but on the course our country will take.

Please know I'm grateful for all you do, and I wish you the very best.

Sincerely,

Barack Obama

WWW.WHITEHOUSE.GOV